LET THEM COME

A Nouthetic Approach to Counseling Youth

by

Felisa McQueen-Lawson

Trafford Publishing Inc.

All scripture quotations are taken from the *Authorized King James Version* of the Bible

A cataloguing record for this book that includes the U.S. Library of Congress Classification number, the Library of Congress Call number and the Dewey Decimal cataloguing code is available from the National Library of Canada. The complete cataloguing record can be obtained from the National Library's online database at: www.nlc-bnc.ca/amicus/index-e.html
ISBN: 1-4120-3032-3

TRAFFORD

This book was published *on-demand* **in cooperation with Trafford Publishing.** On-demand publishing is a unique process and service of making a book available for retail sale to the public taking advantage of on-demand manufacturing and Internet marketing. **On-demand publishing** includes promotions, retail sales, manufacturing, order fulfilment, accounting and collecting royalties on behalf of the author.

Suite 6E, 2333 Government St., Victoria, B.C. V8T 4P4, CANADA

Phone	250-383-6864	Toll-free	1-888-232-4444 (Canada & US)
Fax	250-383-6804	E-mail	sales@trafford.com
Web site	www.trafford.com	TRAFFORD PUBLISHING IS A DIVISION OF TRAFFORD HOLDINGS LTD.	
Trafford Catalogue #04-0859		www.trafford.com/robots/04-0859.html	

10   9   8   7   6   5   4   3   2   1

This book is dedicated to

all those who desire a closer

relationship with GOD, the Creator

and Jesus Christ, His Son

And

To Jerris,

my inspiration,

and the fire that kept

the candle burning

Love ya

ACKNOWLEDGMENTS

I would like to first acknowledge Christ Jesus, who is the head of my life, for I know with Him, all things are possible.

To my husband David, for standing by my side and being ever so patient. Thank you honey. I love you.

To my mother Shirley, who believed in me when I did not believe in myself, I love you. XOXOXOXO

Then to my pastor and Overseer, Elder Dr. Charles B. McCloud, III and his family, including the church family, Mt. Carmel Deliverance Center, for imparting the desire to learn and do as God would have me to do. May blessings flow.

Next, to Dr. Abe Johnson, my mentor and colleague, his wife Mittie, and all the Smith Chapel Bible College family, for encouragement, persistence, and perfection, and bringing the revelation that, *"Students taught by the Holy Spirit study scripture."* May God continue to use you in a mighty way.

And then last, but not lest, to my family, church family, friends, and coworkers for all your support and confidence. Thank you.

TABLE OF CONTENTS

ABOUT THE AUTHOR

Felisa McQueen-Lawson was born in Arcadia, Florida and raised in Rochester, New York, where she graduated from Thomas Jefferson High School with High Honors and was the class Valedictorian. Felisa is Co-Founder and Co-Pastor of Urban Assault Ministries, Inc (Temple of Praise) located in Sneads, Florida. She has a Bachelor and Master Degree from Smith Chapel Bible College (SCBC), and is a Doctoral Candidate (May 2004), of the same. She also serves as an Associate Professor and is Dean of the School of Nouthetic Counseling at SCBC. Felisa is a Board Certified Faith Based Clinical Therapist and has memberships with the American Association of Christian Counselors and the National Association of Faith Based Counselors. She is married to David (Pastor), and is the mother of one son, the late Calvin J. McQueen.

Other Books by this Author

Prerequisites for an Effective Ministry in Nouthetic Counseling

It's Not Your Fault: Spiritual Effects of Incest

Contact Information

Felisa McQueen-Lawson

P.O. Box 717

Sneads, Florida 32460

1-800-579-4UAM

PREFACE

Evidence from television and news articles suggests that due to the mindset of today's young people, crime rates have increased drastically. This research has come about to focus on the mindset or mental status of our youth. We have heard of two boys, seven years of age, committing sodomy and then killing a little boy, three years of age. We have heard of two teenage brothers brutally shooting their parents to death. We also hear of adolescent girls selling their bodies on the street. However, what stands out the most is the increasing number of gangs. Many of the members range in age from eight to eighteen. Each ethnicity has its own gangs, so that tells me, that many of our youth, no matter what race or creed, are experiencing many of the same problems.

So often, we try to correct a spiritual problem with a secular resolution. I believe what happens in the spirit realm, will reveal itself in the natural or physical realm. Therefore, a spiritual problem requires correction by spiritual means. In 2 Timothy 3:16 of the Authorized King James Version of the Bible that, *"All Scripture is given by inspiration of God, and is profitable for doctrine, for reproof, for correction, for instruction in righteousness:"*

During this research, I have come to discover that many of our youth are seeking answers and solutions to their questions and problems. Yet, no one has the suitable and lasting resolution. Our youth today are troublesome because many grow up too fast, others have a lack of nurturing family ties. Then there are others, who just exist, not knowing what their purpose is in life. We as the church, as well as the parent have a duty to our young people. As representatives of Christ Jesus, we have the task of planting good seeds in the lives of every individual we meet. This includes the lives of our young people. They are the nation of tomorrow. Therefore, sound doctrine, not dogma, must come forth now. We have to make an alternative, radical and drastic change to the way we communicate with our young people today. We have to approach them with the truth. I believe the best way to reach our youth is through Nouthetic Counseling, [which will be defined in Chapter 2], verses traditional secular counseling, i.e. psychiatry, psychology. Secular counseling puts the youth in the hands of the world, whereas Nouthetic counseling puts them in the hands of God.

During my search of trying to find other related studies about biblical counseling versus secular counseling for the youth, I found little. Most of the literature I found, including the **DSM-III-R** for Psychiatric Disorders, only gave a description of signs and symptoms of disorders such as Conduct or Behavior Disorder, Post Traumatic Stress Disorder, Attention Deficit Disorder, and so on.

That's all well fine and good, but what is the **'root'** of all this mayhem? What is **causing** the problems? Why are our children subjected to sexual abuse? Why are they raising their younger brothers and sisters? Why is there such a high rate of teen pregnancy? Why are young boys dealing drugs? Why are so many involved in gangs? Why are our young people running away from home? Why are they so hurt and angry? Why are they not in church? The answer is simple. SIN is the root that these young people's problems are stemming from. It is either by their own hand or by the hand of another individual. Most of the literature that I have stumbled on did not address this cause in the lives of our youth. However, the Holy Bible, the Word of God does address this cause and every issue known to man and has a resolution.

PART ONE

The Plan

Chapter ONE

Welcome to the War Zone

"*Breaking News: On the West Coast, two teenagers have just entered a high school, opened fire, killing several students and teachers, using automatic weapons. On the East Coast, a ten year old boy has sodomized and killed a three year old boy. A twelve year old gang leader was brutally killed in a drive by shooting in the north east region. A sixteen year old girl was arrested last night for prostitution. She reports that she had to make money to support her two younger brothers and baby sister. She also reported that both her parents are drug addicts."*

What is happening in today's society to cause so much anger, hatred, violence, and degrading attitudes and behaviors among the youth? Obviously, there is some underlying problem, that is causing such turmoil in the lives of our young people. So, that brings the question as to who is responsible to take on the task of reaching out to our youth, and how does it get done.

As I have already mentioned, we have an influx of young people with various problems, classified as social, mental or behavioral. Granted, some of these problems may be organic, however, most stemmed from some act of sin, known or unknown. I have also mentioned that many of our young people are both hurting and angry. So what have we done to correct this problem? As I began my research and approached several young people aged 9-16, and asked, "Why haven't you gone to talk to your pastor or someone in the church?". Their response was, "I can't go to the pastor because he won't listen" or "they [the church] won't let me say anything" or "they say I'm not old enough to be experiencing any *real* problems, wait until I have grown up and then *we* can talk". I then asked several preachers and others in leadership positions within the church, "Are you counseling your young people, and if not why?" Their response was this; "I don't know how to approach them [youth]"; or "They're too young to understand God's Word. They must wait until they're old enough to understand"; or "they won't listen to anything I have to say." What's wrong with this picture? Our youth have a serious need. They are asking for help, yet we fail to recognize the cry. So what do we do? We ignore them, and that is what sends them off into a tie raid or off the deep end.

We only recognize a problem when it is publicized all over national television, for example, Columbine High School or the Menendez murders. We focus on the issues that bring national attention, but what about the problems occurring in our own states, our own communities, and in our own backyards. We as the church, as the community, need to reach out to our young people and 'let them come'. Even Jesus of Nazareth, in his ministry, took time with the youth. As it is written in Matthew 19: 14, He said, *"Suffer little children, and forbid them not, to come unto me: for of such is the kingdom of heaven."*

Chapter TWO

What is Nouthetic Counseling?

Nouthetic Counseling is simply Bible based or Scripture based counseling. Nouthetic comes from the Greek word *'nouthesia'*, which means, "training by the word", whether of encouragement, reproof or remonstrance. Nouthetic Counseling counterattacks any problem or situation caused by sin, either known or unknown, by bringing it under subjection to the Truth. Clients/counselees are given a choice to either, continue in sin or allow God's Truth through the Holy Scriptures, bring them to a point of release and freedom. Likewise, what makes this form of counseling unique is the counselor uses *only* the Word of God, while relying on the Holy Spirit to give revelation and understanding of written scriptures.

You may have asked, "What makes Nouthetic Counseling different?" Let me use the following analogy.

*You have a toaster that is not working properly. How do you know that it is not working properly? Well you realize that the bread is not browning as it should. In other words, you **know** the toaster is not doing what it was **designed** to do. How ever, in order for the toaster to be fixed, you must send it to the manufacturer. The*

manufacturer designed the toaster and knows
exactly *how to resolve the problem. When all is said and done, the problem was* **not** *the fact that the bread was not browning. The* **real** *problem was there was a burned out element in the toaster.*

So, as it is with Nouthetic Counseling. God the Creator designed man (mankind). He is the only one who knows exactly what the problem is and how to fix it.

Counseling youth today requires truth, fact, and straightforwardness. Many have serious issues that have to be dealt with head on. Only God knows how to solve the problem. It is by His Word that a young person will come to understand why they exist, why they are going through such turmoil, and what it is that God has in store for them .

Chapter THREE

PREREQUISITES FOR A NOUTHETIC COUNSELER

Nouthetic counseling is an awesome ministry[1], in that one has to stay in constant contact with God. Just as the Holy Spirit guides and directs the pastor/counselor, then also should the counselor guide and direct the counselee while depending on the Holy Spirit. Nouthetic counseling is a ministry that can truly change lives. It causes to counselee to come to terms with the real problem at hand. Any problem can be solved, by applying

---

[1] For more details of this chapter, read my book *Prerequisites for Effective Ministry in Nouthetic Counseling*

God's Word. God uses the counselor, to assist the counselee in rightly dividing the Word, so the Word can be understood, put into the right perspective in relation to the problem, and then accomplish the goal by rightly applying the Word to the circumstance. Salvation is at hand. It takes the Word of God to accomplish it.

PREREQUISITES

There should be certain criteria that must be met before anyone delves into nouthetic counseling as a ministry. Can anyone learn nouthetic counseling? Possibly. Can anyone become a nouthetic counselor? Probably not. There are certain prerequisites that a person must and should have prior to becoming a nouthetic counselor. These prerequisites are as follows:

1) wisdom;
2) prayer;
3) fire;
4) hearing God;
5) faith;
6) non judgmental.

Notice the number of prerequisites there are to be a nouthetic counselor. The number is six. In biblical numerics, the number six represents the weakness of man. It is the duty of the nouthetic counselor to bring every counselee, either bond or free, into right standing with God. The counselee should be able to recognize, with the aid of the counselor, while endeavoring into the Word of God and acknowledging and accepting God's standards as their own, the principles that were rejected. Let us look a little closer at these prerequisites.

WISDOM

What is wisdom, why must we have it, how do we get it, and how is it used in counseling? These are legitimate questions with very easy answers. Answers that come from an authoritative resource, The Holy Bible, King James Version, 1611.

What is wisdom? Proverbs 9:10 tells us, *"The fear of the Lord is the beginning of wisdom"*. The fear, meaning *reverence* or *awe*, of the Lord, is the first step or start of acquiring wisdom, which is being able to make sound judgments in any matter, by the way of education, experience, and most profoundly, by the way of the Holy Ghost.

Daniel 2:20 says this, *"Wisdom and might are His"*. Wisdom comes from God the Creator. If wisdom is His, then in order for anyone to attempt to gain knowledge, one must come to know God. We must also note that according to Proverbs 4:7, *"Wisdom is the principal thing; therefore get wisdom: and with all thy getting, get understanding"*, having wisdom is of vital importance. In all things, one must be wise. We must seek God in order to get wisdom. To seek wisdom is to seek God.

Why must we have wisdom? Here is just a short list:

1. *...they shall <u>understand</u> <u>the lovingkindness of the Lord</u>.* Ps. 107:43

2. *Discretion shall preserve thee, understanding shall keep thee.* Prov. 2:11

3. *Happy is the man that findeth wisdom,and..getteth understanding.* Prov. 3:13

4. *She shall bring thee to honour, when thou dost embrace her.* Prov. 4:8

5. *Whoso findeth me findeth life, ... shall obtain favour of the Lord.* Prov. 8:35.

It behooves anyone to take up the quest of attaining the knowledge and understanding of God. Is it an easy task? For many, no. Can it be done? Yes. The promises of God are sure. Ponder on this text, *"The wise man's eyes are in his head; but the fool walketh in darkness"*, Ecclesiastes 2:14.

How do you get wisdom? Easy. Just ask for it. James 1:5 says, *"If any of you lack wisdom, let him ask of God"*. *"Give me now wisdom and knowledge"*, 2 Chronicles 1:10. *"The Lord giveth wisdom: out of His mouth cometh knowledge and understanding"*, Proverbs 2:6. *"Those that seek me early shall find me"*, Proverbs 8:17. Then we have written in Exodus 31:6, *" In the hearts of all that are wise hearted I have put wisdom"*.

Wisdom is there for the asking. God will freely give. Often times people are not trusting when something is offered to them for free. When gives something freely, He gives His best. Look what He did when He gave us His only begotten Son. He offered the world salvation, and many still refuse it.

Now that we know what wisdom is, why we must have it, and how we get it, how is it used in nouthetic counseling? Let us look at two verses of scripture. The first scripture that we will look at is, I Kings 3:9. The scripture reads as this, *"Give therefore thy servant an understanding heart to judge thy people, that I may discern between good and bad: for who is able to judge this thy so great a people?"* This same question should be asked by every counselor before entering into a session with a counselee. The request is simply asking for a discerning spirit, so the counselee would not be judged falsely and/or in turn would not be given bad counsel. Remember wisdom comes from God, therefore all counsel should be godly. Also, realize that we as counselors do not judge, but it's God's Word that convicts a corrupt heart and challenges the individual to either repent or continue to walk in darkness, meaning sin. This leads us to the second scripture.

"*Neither do men put new wine into old bottles: else the bottles break, and the wine runneth out*", Matthew 9:17. Now you may ask, "what does this scripture have to do with wisdom and counseling?" A repentant heart (*new wine*), can not live within a dead spirit (*old bottles*). That which is new cannot stay within the confines of something old, dirty, and is now of none effect. Every nouthetic counselor has the charge of bringing every counselee to the acknowledgment of God's Word, pointing out the errors committed, and leading them by faith, to God by repentance, forgiveness, rededication, and Holy Spirit baptism.

How would you know if one is truly exerting wisdom in their counseling ministry? See if they can pass this test, "*He that winneth*

souls is wise and *A true witness delivereth souls"*,
Proverbs 11:30; 14:25.

PRAYER

"Watch ye therefore, and pray always",
were the words that were spoken by Jesus of
Nazareth, as recorded in Luke 21:36. Jesus is
actually speaking in relation to watching for
the signs of the endtimes. However, I believe
that every counselor, every day, before,
during, and after each counseling session,
should watch and pray, always.

When we pray, we communion, or talk
to God. We worship Him, we petition Him,
we thank Him, and we praise Him. Yet the
one thing we all should do, any many do not,
is to allow time for God to speak to us. When
we pray, it should be a two-way

communication. Jeremiah 33:3 says this, "*Call unto Me, and I will answer thee, and show thee great and mighty things which thou knowest not.*" He desires for His people to commune with Him, but He also wants His people to hear His voice. "*The Lord is nigh unto all them that call upon Him, to all that call upon Him in truth*". What is this saying? It is saying that God can only hear those who are in right standing with Him. In other words, those whom have been redeemed, are they whom He calls sons and daughters. As we draw closer to God, He draws closer to us. It is this example that the counselor should show and express to every counselee.

FIRE

What is the term "fire" in reference to? Fire is in reference to the power of the Holy

Ghost dwelling on inside of man. It is the Holy Ghost that teaches the mind, comforts the soul, warns the body, illuminates the Word of God, and empowers & quickens the spirit of man. One cannot grow in God without God's spirit being the catalyst. The evidence of a Holy Ghost filled person, is the manifestation of holy and righteous living, and the manifestation of love and its attributes as recorded in Galatians 5:22-23. The Holy Ghost is third person of the Godhead, whom the counselor should be **actively** listening to, while in a counseling session. It is the Holy Ghost that will tell the counselor exactly what the problem is, and it is He that will give direction as to what to say to the counselee, what scriptures to read, and how and what to pray concerning the individual. This does not negate the necessity for continued study of the Word of God. In essence, this too is how we hear God.

HEARING GOD

As was previously mentioned, we hear God not only by His Holy Spirit, or in prayer, but also by dreams and visions, and by reading and studying His Word. But, how does one know if it is truly God speaking and it's His voice that is heard? The voice that is heard must be consistent with the written Word of God. This is very key in nouthetic counseling. Why? Well, the counselee will often times come in with some type of sin problem, even though they may try to cover it up or dress it up. The counselor must be able to hear the Holy Spirit speaking, because it is

He that will reveal the real problem and will thereby give the solution to the problem.

We know that as it is written in II Timothy 3: 16, *"All scripture is given by inspiration of God, and is profitable for doctrine, for reproof, for correction, for instruction in righteousness"*. In I John 4:1a it is written, *"Beloved, believe not every spirit, but try the spirits whether they are of God..."*. Now, if the counselor is not in right standing with the Father, and has not sought a relationship with the Son, then the Holy Spirit can not be heard, and Satan will have control of the counseling session and therefore ungodly counsel will be given. It is imperative that godly counsel be given, because lives are at stake, spiritual and natural. It is the duty of the nouthetic counselor to steer the counselee to Christ, not away from Him.

FAITH

How is faith obtained? The Apostle Paul told the believers in Rome, *"That faith cometh by hearing and hearing by the word of God"*, Romans 10:17. Faith comes by hearing the Word of God.

What is faith? Hebrews 11:1 says this, *"Now faith is the substance of things hoped for, the evidence of things not seen"*. I interpret this verse this way, faith is the surety and expectation of knowing that something that is not currently tangible, will at a later time become a reality. I also believe that faith is having a trust in someone or something that cannot be seen or heard in the physical or natural scheme of things. Faith goes beyond the usual and ordinary.

The Bible also tells us in the book of Hebrews 11:6, *"But without faith it is impossible to please him: for he that cometh to God must believe that he is, and that he is a rewarder of them that diligently seek him."* A nouthetic counselor has to believe that that God can change any circumstance and anybody, and this same belief has to be evident to the counselee. If the counselor can stand on God's Word, then the counselee has to be challenged to do the same.

NON JUDGMENTAL

One point in nouthetic counseling, in which I believe is a critical point, is that the counselor has to be nonjudgmental. Jesus of Nazareth states, as it is written in John 7:24, *"Judge not according to the appearance, but judge righteous judgment"*. So what if the counselee is a drunkard, or a prostitute, or denies God totally. With the Word, good counsel, and the conviction by the Holy Spirit, anyone can change, **if** the counselee is willing to change. God has a plan and purpose for every individual. It is not to be determined by the counselor if any is *fit* to be redeemed or justified by God. We must remember that there was a time when we too were bound by sin, and yet God say it fit to redeem us, only after we allowed His Son to be Lord and Savior of our lives. This is the message that has to be relayed to everyone, not just those whom we counsel, but everyone, in which we come in contact.

Chapter FOUR

A.G.A.P.E.
A Christian model for counseling

The theoretical model that God has given me to use has this acronym, **A.G.A.P.E.**, Godly love. It is my belief that a counselor must give an example and express a love that goes beyond understanding. It's a love that only God shows and by His Spirit working in the counselor, I believe the counselee will be able to feel this love. It is easy for anyone to open themselves in a counseling session when they know that someone really and truly is concerned about their well- being, not just their physical well-being but their spiritual well-being. Once you tap into the spirit of man, and rectify the problem therein, the body will follow suit.

The A.G.A.P.E. model will always bring the counselor and the counselee in to a frame of mind to be open, honest, nonjudgmental, and maintain the atmosphere of God's unconditional love. Let's examine the model.

A – **assess** what the counselee tells you (symptoms, subjective), then with reliance on The Holy Spirit, make an **analysis** bringing the problem to the forefront.

G – together determine the **goal** or what the expected outcome should be, staying within the boundaries of God's Word and direction (principle).

A – **approach** the goal by **application** of God's   Word to correct the problem.

P – **practice** by reciting scriptures several times a day, allowing the words to become life and breath in the heart and spirit; keep a daily journal; attend all counseling sessions (individual – 1:1, may also include group sessions if necessary); develop and instill prayer sessions (individual and family); attend weekly church services as often as possible.

E – **evaluate** the progress of the counselee by maintaining counseling sessions as scheduled; document demeanor, facial expressions, context and content of discussion (positive, negative, stuck on the past, discuss future, etc…), repentance, deliverance, salvation, Holy Ghost baptism, rededication.

In any counseling arena, there is no sure time frame as to how long a counselee will remain in counseling. I truly believe that the time spent in counseling, depends on the counselee's willingness and determination to heal, be delivered and set free from the bondage that holds them captive.

The **A.G.A.P.E.** model, if used accurately and consistently, will prove to be yet another effective counseling tool for solving any problem nouthetically. It's design has been made so that anyone from Pastor to layperson, should be able to grasp the concept and fulfill the call of 'making disciples' and expand the family of God.

PART TWO

Unmasking the Problem

Chapter FIVE

Approaching Our Youth

Some adults claim it is impossible to talk to teenagers. Some parents have said that their child is too young to understand matters of the heart. Some teachers say that a particular child won't ever amount to anything because he/she is so unruly now. Look at what has just happened. Already, the child has been degraded, belittled, and berated before he/she can get a good start in life. Just because the child may be under the age of eighteen, does not mean that they cannot understand what is being said to them, if it is said in a way that they can comprehend.

Youth today want to know that they have a voice. They want to know that when they have an opinion or ask for help, it will not fall on deaf ears. They want to feel loved and needed. But, most importantly, they want to know the truth. There is but one truth, that is the Word of God. Only God can counteract what Satan has done through the vise of sin.

However, as counselors we must understand and come to terms with the problems the youth are facing in today's society. The following chapters will pinpoint some of the major problems our youth are facing and the cause. It is my prayer that after reading the next few chapters, that you the reader, will view our young people in a different light, and begin to realize that we do have a problem. We must remember that at one time, we too were five, ten, and fifteen years old. Some of the same problems we faced growing up are now possibly ten times worse. As adults, we are held responsible and accountable, by God, for the training of our youth.

.

Chapter SIX

Train Up a Child

The Bible tells us in Proverbs 22:6, *"Train up a child in the way he should go: and when he is old, he will not depart from it."* In plain English, this verse tells us that we are to nurture, motivate, instruct, and discipline our youth concerning the nature and things of God. Should the child as an adult depart from a godly lifestyle, as he grows old, he will remember those things which were taught to him at an earlier age.

Well, if this is the case, then why have our youth at such an early age gone astray?

In the book of Deuteronomy 6:7, the Lord God, through Moses, commanded the children of Israel to obey his commandments and statutes, and to teach them diligently unto their children, and talk of them, when they sit in the house, when they walk by the way, when they lie down, and when they rise up. I believe that we too, must do the same.

Chapter SEVEN

Sins of the Father

Acts of sin are passed down from generation to generation. Therefore the term "sins of the father", now becomes known as generational curses. Curses are manifested by rebellion. Rebellion from what? Rebellion from the knowledge and obedience to God the Creator. Daniel 9:5 of the Bible says this, *"We have sinned, and have committed iniquity, and have done wickedly, and have rebelled, even by departing from thy precepts and from thy judgements."*

If the only thing that our children see is violence, day in and day out, they will presume that it is okay, and that everyone experiences it. Our children are very impressionable, and observant. They will say the things you say, and do the things you do. In order for us to train up a child in the way he should go, we as the parents, adults, mentors, etc., must be the prime example of living a life of holiness and righteousness. Yes, we will make mistakes, but that's why it is written that we must strive for perfection and repent daily.

Children can be abused in as many ways as the adult victim. There is the obvious physical abuse such as pinching, hitting, twisting arms, etc.; sexual abuse which is usually incestual or by a close family friend; intimidation such as instilling fear, being violent towards a pet, yelling, etc.; isolation from peers, grandparents, siblings, or another parent; using threats like suicide, abandonment, harm to a loved one, etc.; using institutions as a threat like the police, foster home, jail, mental institutions, God, etc.; and there is the emotional abuse like name calling, put downs, spying on the other parent, being inconsistent, and shaming the child. How many of us have experienced these things, and probably have done these things and not realized that we were being abused or abusive? In many Christian homes, children are taught to honor thy father and mother, and to obey your parents. In my household, the common phrase was, "Do as I say, not as I do."

Children are not stupid. A statement like that simply implies that the parent is not doing what he/she should be doing. Children often learn by hearing and observing, wanting to be like daddy, wanting to be like mommy. They understand what it is to be good, but if all they see is bad, and that is not dealt with and corrected, then yes, they will grow in the way that they have been trained. They will grow up to be VIOLENT, INCONSIDERATE, UNTRUSTWORTHY, and UNGODLY. Thus, we have the generational curse.

A generational curse will linger until someone in the generational line, recognizes the sin in their life, repent and be reconciled to God, ask Christ Jesus to be the Lord and Savior of their life, get sanctified by the blood, crucified by the Word, calls that violent spirit and every other demonic spirit associated with it, to come out, and is totally delivered, and then get baptized and filled with the Holy Ghost, that he may walk in the Spirit, and live by the Spirit, having a life of peace, joy, and happiness, living holy and righteous.

Chapter EIGHT

Grown Up too Soon

As Christians living in today's vile society, we MUST explain to our children that it is wrong for ANYBODY to touch them inappropriately. We often tell them that sex is for grownups, but not being specific in saying, THAT SEX IS FOR A GROWNUP MAN AND A GROWNUP WOMAN WHO ARE MARRIED TO EACH OTHER. Then and only then is sex appropriate. And again, yes many of us have made mistakes, but we have to be able to explain to the child that when two people come together, in a sexual way, that the two become as one. WE as Christians have to understand, that there is a transference of spirits when the two come together, whether it is consensual or not, no matter what the age.

Concerning sexual abuse, statistics show that 1 in 4 girls and 1 in 7 boys, will have been molested at least once by the age of 18. Most often, the abuser is someone the child knows. Whether it is a blood relative (incest), or someone close to the family (friend). Signs of sexual abuse vary, depending on the age of the child at the onset, how long the abuse occurred in regards to months or years, and the relation of the abuser to the child.

When someone abuses a child in a sexual way, a host of spirits can transfer to that child, such as: lust, shame, guilt, depression, promiscuity, anger, fear, suicide, homicide, self-mutilation, and multiple personality disorder, and so many others. If you know that a woman is being abused in a relationship, please, please watch and keep a close eye on the children.

What about when it comes to disciplining our children? How many of you have used the phrase, "Spare the rod, spoil the child"? Is this really scriptural? Let's take a look.

Proverbs 13:24, *"He that spareth his rod hateth his son: but he who loveth him* chasteneth *him betimes."* The rod is figurative for guidance and direction. Many have misinterpreted this verse of scripture because they take the rod to be literal. And he who loves him is the one that diligently disciplines the son early. We are to guide, direct, teach, protect, and above all, love our children. Not use, hurt, and abuse them.

Let's go back and look at Ephesians 6:1-4.

Ephesians 6:1; *Children, obey your parents in the Lord*: meaning those parents who have a relationship with God for they are His representatives: *for this is right.* Ephesians 6:2,3; *Honour thy father and mother*; (esteem and value); *which is the first commandment with promise; that it may be well with thee, and thou mayest live long on the earth.*

Ephesians 6:4; *And, ye fathers, provoke not your children to wrath ,* (meaning anger and resentment): *but bring them up in the nurture and admonition* (meaning; training, counsel, discipline, and correction/warning) *of the Lord.*

PART THREE

The Solution

Chapter NINE

New Heights

There are four reasons why secular counseling programs tend to fail the youth: 1) cost, 2) geographical location, 3) trust, and 4) life changing experience.

Secular programs are costly. On average the cost per counseling session with a psychologist or psychiatrist is $150.00 (one hundred fifty dollars). Most clients are required to see the psychologist/psychiatrist at least once a week. This totals to $600.00 (six hundred dollars) a month.

Most families with low income do not have the resources to pay out this kind of money every month. So counseling goes lacking. In some cases, insurance will foot the bill. But, once again a family with low income, probably doesn't have insurance for health care.

The majority of secular counseling centers, and offices are not located within a rural area. People that live in rural areas are often reluctant to come into the 'city'. However, most secular counselors or professionals will not go to the client.

Many young people are very cautious and will not readily trust someone they don't know. In most circumstances, this is good because it serves as a defense mechanism. Yet, in a counseling situation, it can be a hindrance. To gain the trust of a young person, respect and a caring attitude towards them must be demonstrated by the counselor.

Then there is the life changing experience or lack thereof. An individual has to change from the inside out. In other words, the spirit man has to change. Only by the Word of God, which is truth, can an individual change. II Corinthians 5:17 says this, *"Therefore any man be in Christ, he is a new creature: old things are passed away; behold, all things are become new."* Secular counseling restricts the use of any spiritual teaching. Now is the time for the church, pastors, church leaders, Christian counselors and parents to step up to the plate. It is up to us to train our youth, gain their trust, get them back on the right track, and most importantly, allow them to be what they are, young people.

We (adults) have an obligation, a well as the parents, to protect our young people. Due to their age, and innocence, youth are much more susceptible of being caught in and bound by an unwanted, unwarranted situation of which they have no control. We have to step in and pray, talk, counsel, and love these younger ones, if for whatever reason the parent/(s) cannot.

What else can we do to help our youth?:

1) develop recreational activities after school,

2) have bible studies, rap/talk sessions,

3) plan events including other churches; musicals, bowling, skating, talent/fashion shows, dance troop, etc…

CONCLUSION

Nouthetic Counseling serves as an alternative approach to counsel our youth. It does not cost anything, it can be used in any geographical location or setting. It's perfect for counselors, clergy, and parents.

Nouthetic Counseling brings forth truth and unmasks the wiles of sin. Our youth deserve a fighting chance in life to succeed, prosper, and live happy and healthy. But, they also deserve to know who they are in God. They deserve to know that someone out there does love them and care about them. They deserve to know that they don't have to live a life of shame, disgust, hurt, and torment. They too are God's children. All they need is a chance. A chance to come and be heard. A chance to come and cry. LET THEM COME.

REFERENCES

Adams, Jay E. *Competent to Counsel.*
Michigan: Zondervan, 1970

Banks, Bill, and Sue Banks. *Breaking Unhealthy Soul-Ties.*
Kirkwood: Impact Christian Books, Inc., 1999

Buckley, Ed. *Why Christians Can't Trust Psychology.*
Oregon: Harvest House Publishers, 1993

Flannery Jr., Raymond B. *Preventing Youth Violence.*
New York: The Continuum Publishing Company, 1999

Fogarty, James A. *The Magical Thoughts of Grieving Children.*
New York: Baywood Publishing Company, Inc., 2000

Golden, Larry B. *Case Studies in Child and Adolescent Counseling.*
New Jersey: Merrill Prentice Hall, 2002

Heitritter, Lynn, and Jeanette Vought. *Helping Victims of Sexual Abuse.* Minnesota: Bethany House Publishers, 1989

James, John W., and Russell Friedman. *When Children Grieve.*
New York: Harper Collins Publishers, 2001

Rowatt Jr., G. Wade. *Adolescents in Crisis.*
Kentucky: Westminster John Knox Press, 2001

Strong, James. *The New Strong's Complete Dictionary of Bible Words.* Nashville: Thomas Nelson Publishers, 1996

Vine, W. E., and Merrill F. Unger, and William White, Jr., *Vine's Complete Expository Dictionary of Old and New Testament Words.*
Nashville: Thomas Nelson Publishers, 1985

ISBN 1412030323

Made in the
USA
Middletown, DE